ANTHOLOGY OF A TWENTIETH CENTURY MAN

To
Beryl & Robert
Warmest good wishes
from
Tom. Kelly

Anthology of a Twentieth Century Man

TOM KELLY

Serendipity

First published in 2003 by
Serendipity
Suite 530
37 Store Street
Bloomsbury
London
WC1E 7QF

British Library Cataloguing-in-Publication data
A catalogue record for this book is availalbe from the British Library

ISBN 1–84394–060–4

Printed and bound in the United Kingdom by the Alden Group, Oxford

In memory of my dearly beloved wife Jean
(1926–2002)

Contents

About the Author

In some of his work the author, now in his eighty-first year, has endeavoured to shed a little light on the lifestyle and nature of man in the twentieth century.

He has lived through a number of years that equate to well over three-quarters of the period; soldiered as an artillery man throughout the Second World War, seen paraffin lamps and gas light give way to electricity, and the development of electronics. He has witnessed the advent of radio, television, and computers; the progression from mainly horse drawn vehicles to modern modes of transport, amidst a multitude of many scientific and engineering developments, not discounting the awesome atomic and nuclear bombs; and he feels that with the passing of the years some features of his work will have an element of historical value. For this reason he has chosen to wear his heart upon his sleeve, and display his feelings in this little book.

Author's Notes

As expressed in the opening poem anyone disposed to writing prose or verse will no doubt be aware that such activity is often an exposition of their innermost psyche; a wearing of one's heart upon the sleeve so to speak.

Such a pastime is not an exhibition of dogma, it is simply a need to express one's thoughts and to share them with others. To do so is to shed all inhibitions and in the process hope that those who enjoy sharing their thoughts do so without attaching to the poet terms of egoism or extroversion.

To those who are averse to some expressed thoughts the writer feels he has not penned words in vain, for he realises that such aversion can become a platform for intelligent debate; such dialogue can only lead to a union of thoughts, or a friendly failure to agree. Either way the written words will have generated food for thought and exercised the mind.

In this anthology the reader will find a variety of expressed thoughts, some triggered by incidents or relationships, others by reflections of the past. The latter are the product, and perhaps the prerogative of the aged mind. They will also find lyrics of songs and hymns that are the companions of the writer's musical compositions. It is the expressed hope that individually these will prompt a variety of thoughts and moods, and collectively win favour with the reader.

Sometimes pensive, sometimes humorous, sometimes reflective, sometimes advisory, within these pages the reader will find a public exposition of one man's soul. Individual items of his work have been published with commendations, but this is the first occasion that a collection of his work has been given an airing. Many a reader, especially in maturity will, it is hoped, find an affinity with a great deal of the writer's expressed thoughts for they are, indeed, a portrait of life as experienced by an ordinary man throughout most of the twentieth century.

To a Poet – a Kindred Spirit

We who in this life do choose
To disdain material gain,
Simply pen emotions, thoughts
Seeking not a path to fame.
Nor do we hanker for great wealth,
Or names ablaze in lights.
We kindred souls seek simply
A healthy happy life.
Tranquillity of mind and heart
Enjoyed when expressed thought
Appears alive on vellum,
This can't be sold or bought
By those who seek to profit
From a soul that one lays bare.
Sufficient pleasure is derived
When folk like us can share
With others, words of wisdom,
Of truth and sanity,
For unlike any other form of art
There for all to see
Is not the sculptured model,
Nor the masterpiece enframed,
But man's soul, his very spirit
An ever-burning flame
That shines upon the written words
In hope that all can see
We who pen them, simply try,
To set our spirit free.

Slim's Forgotten 14th Army

'When you go home tell them of us and say,
"For your tomorrow we gave our today".'

Through jungles' steamy heat they fought,
Through torrential rains; forded angry rivers,
Baked by the sun, ravaged by malaria,
Heroes everyone, their noble deeds unsung
They were Uncle Bill's Forgotten Army.

Orde Wingate's Chindits humped bent low
Beneath their backpacks, foot slogging
Warriors with arms unslung, bayonets fixed
Heroes each and every one.
Nerves stretched to break, sinews taut,
Behind the enemy lines they fought.
They were Uncle Bill's Forgotten Army.

At Arakan and Imphal, and the tennis court Kohima,
Bloody battles waged and won,
With Indian troops and Ghurkas they
Bridged the Chindwin, forded the Irrawady
To put the 'Slant Eyes' on the run,
And down the road to Mandalay
They were Uncle Bill's Forgotten Army.

On the road from Mandalay taking Toungoo
And Pegu the Fourteenth Army fought its way,
Ere before the second monsoon
With Jap resistance all the way
They came and took Rangoon, 'twas the third of May
In nineteen-forty-five; some came back alive.
They were Uncle Bill's Forgotten Army.

Back unto their homeland came the 'Phantom Brigade',
Unheralded; in silence; no fanfares,
Nor flags or bunting waved; unsung heroes
No one raved on their return.
They were Uncle Bill's Forgotten Army.

Faraway Places (The One Who Got Away)

It was late in nineteen-forty,
The war was in its second year,
I'd had six months in London's bombing,
And still trembled with fear.

Then came a single posting,
To Perch Rock in New Brighton
To join a draft for the Far East,
I did not think it fun.

Tropical kit was issued,
And with it came vaccination,
Then we moved to Blundell Sands,
All set for embarkation.

Suddenly one morning
I could not get out of bed,
With body aching head to toe
I lay like a lump of lead.

Wrapped in a rough grey blanket
In the arms of a strong MO
I was carted off in an army truck,
To the 29th Hospital Ormskirk, and so,

They treated me for cowpox
Brought on by vaccination,
And that is how I came to miss
A Far East embarkation.

VE Day

Yes, faster than the eye can blink
Quicker than the mind can think
Fifty years have swept away
Since VE Day, the eighth of May.
Time now for us to celebrate,
And equally commemorate
Those who gave their lives that we
Who came home are still alive, and free.

Yes older memories appear so clear
Of comrades, friends, no longer here.
School kids I fought with down the lanes,
Teenage pals lost in their planes,
Killed in battle, drowned at sea,
I shall not forget their names,
They're branded in the memory.

I knew them from the age of three
We grew up in Mynachdy,
A tight knit, close community.
Norman, Tommy, Ralph and Sidney
And Ivor Mac, and Shorty Jack,
And Les, and Bert and Fred.
They did not as I come back,
They count among our Glorious Dead.

Nine names amidst the multitude
That linger in the memory.
Think on this, enjoy the fun,
And think of every Mother's Son
Who died fighting for liberty,
Who cannot share the Victory

Stood in silence on VE Day
Remember them with me, and pray
That ne'er again you'll ever see
Such a waste of youth, such misery.

Rambling Septuagenarian Thoughts

Tasks that took no time at all
Take ages now, drive one up the wall,
Arms appear to get shorter and shorter,
Or is the floor so far away?
Eyes that once could read a licence plate
From seventy feet away,
Now struggle to differentiate
The night time from the day.

Time was, when one could hear a mouse squeak,
A whispered speak, a floor board creak,
Time now, one would not hear a cannon roar
A creaking floor, a banging door.
A nose that once could smell a rose,
Fresh baked bread, or unwashed hair
Is now a proboscis veined by booze
That sniffs in rank polluted air.

Reminding one of childhood days
When mighty horses towed the drays,
And a tiny pony pulled a trap.
When milkmen fed their horses hay,
And streets were filled with equestrian crap,
And Dad yelled loud 'Get out there son
Here's bucket and shovel, collect that dung'
Which he'd spread on his garden with great care
Over rose beds, rhubarb, mint and mustard.
Oh yes, I remember all so well,
For the kids next door would sniff, and yell
'When we have rhubarb, we have custard.'

Now that I have time to spare
There are some memories I can share,
A million stories I could tell
Of childhood days when all seemed well,
When eyes were clear, and ears could hear
When nose could smell, and tongue could tell
The difference 'tween margarine and butter,
And flexible fingers could flick with ease
Marbles and alleys in the gutter.

Very well can I recall 'ciggy' cards
Stood up by a wall; with supreme skill
I'd knock them down; as with
Conkers on a string, strike hard
Strike fast, and play to win.
That's how it was inside the Ring
Just three rounds of bob, and weave,
What's this guy got up his sleeve?
Dodge his straight left, hook with right,
Back him up, short lefts with sting
Grit one's teeth, and fight to win.
Let him know he's in a fight,
Fight to win, old Pop did say
And if you lose, just walk away
There'll always be another day.

Playing 'Rugger' for the school
Blind side 'Prop' in the front row,
Field in Rumney white with snow
Ball in hand, and shoved by pack,
Crossed the try line, mighty crack,
Under the snow a hidden stone
Out like a light concussed and prone,
Came around contused, confused
Did we win or did we lose?
Came the answer 'Yes we won,
And you played a blinder son'.
That's high praise when one is small,
Makes you feel you are ten foot tall.

Such youthful memories flood the mind
Pictures formed are bright and clear,
Now old, bemused; it's so unkind,
'What did I have for breakfast dear?'
And her indoors says 'Toasted bread,
God knows what that rock did to your head,
And what about the punch you took
From Billy Donoghue's hard right hook
That laid you out for far too long.'
'Yes dear, that was my sad swan song.'

And now 'tis the winter of discontent
Arthritic knees, cold fingers bent,
Joints are aching, back is breaking,
Don't sleep too well, and tired on waking,
So far removed from youthful years
When unblocked tear ducts shed real tears,
When blood flowed free through arteries,
And a healthy heart tick-tocked with ease.
When life was filled with mysteries,
And calf-love triggered trembling knees.
When romance blossomed, and then died,
And unblocked tear ducts cried and cried.
Were teenage years so full of fun?
Can youth be wasted on the young?
To those who ask, I simply say
I'd welcome back most every day
Make haste slowly, that's what I say
To the foolhardy young
Who wish their lives away.

Still Rambling

Faster than the eye can blink
Quicker than the mind can think,
Time flits by.
Older memories appear so clear
With each and every passing year.
Quite like when very small
Yesterday's memories simple to recall.
Now maths, and things that teachers taught
Are lost in mists of tangled thought.

Ask me now of yesteryear
Yes, older memories are very clear.
Of middle age, of early wedded bliss,
Of teenage years, of that first kiss.
Songs of my youth, my puberty
The toddling stage of infancy.
Big warm and cuddly teddy bear,
The old oak, rocking, wheeled highchair

Paraffin lamplight, fumes and smell,
Coal-fired stove remembered well,
Stew pot forever on the hob,
Dad's search for that elusive job.
Sisters and brothers arriving from heaven,
Two, three, four, five, six then seven.
Bath nights in the old tin tub,
Giving siblings' backs a scrub.
Carbolic smell of soap bright red,
Fairy stories, then to bed.

Off to school, just gone three,
Rough grey trousers to the knee.
Legs chafed by winter rain,
Fingers cold and stiff with pain.
All the teachers through the years,
Playground games, lane fights and tears.
Black garbed nuns, full of grace,
Swishing cane, tear-stained face.
Infants-primary-standard seven,
Failed for high school, aged eleven.

Long-trousered, restless, callow youth
Bum-fluffed face, raw, uncouth,
Pubic hair, and acned skin,
The brash veneer, the fear within.
Mans' world out there, yet unseen,
Met head on when just fourteen.
A job to do, a trade to learn,
A time to grow, a wage to earn.
Three half-crowns, the first weekend,
Two for Mam, and one to spend.
Meeting girls at Roath Park Rec,
Study nights at Cardiff Tech.
Holidays down 'Bare Bum Bay',
Carefree hours of youth at play.
Big Band days of dance and swing,
Seventy-eights of dear old 'Bing'.

'Peace in our time', Chamberlain said,
Six long years we count our dead.
Not yet eighteen, off to war,
No longer callow youth, and raw
We'll teach you how to fight my son,
And this my lad we call a gun.
Keep it clean, maintain it well
It'll be your friend out there in hell.

Youthful days fast put to flight,
Replaced by manhood overnight.
Bing replaced by Vera Lynn,
Ration books, and snoek in tin.
Queues for this and that in Blighty,
Hitler's conquering power almighty,
Europe falling in defeat,
Countries ravished at his feet.

Dunkirk, Europe's Waterloo
Revived spirit by 'The Few'.
Britain bombed by day and night,
Churchill's speeches – beacons bright.
Orations spouted with élan,
Calling every fighting man,
In sky, on land, and on the sea
To overcome the enemy.

Come 'D-day' the sixth of June,
Past midnight, there was no moon
Five thousand vessels – human cargo,
Answering Ike's 'OK let's go'.
GIs beached at Utah,
Scaling cliffs at Omaha
Beaches Juno, Sword, and Gold
Assailed by young men, fast grown old.

Warriors from the USA,
Polish paladins in the fray,
Youth of Canada, UK, and France
Led the 'Jerry' quite a dance.
Through Normandy, across the Seine they swept,
And sisters, wives and mothers wept
As daily telegrams arrived,
Your husband, father, son has died.

Reflections of the Aged, and Advice to the Young

Fifty years have quickly flown
Since first your Nan and I were wed
And if you think each day was bliss
You each are off your tiny head,
For oft times we both worried
About rationing and money
Those times in early post-war days
You'd hardly call them funny.
No, they were dark and dismal times,
OK, the war was done,
But for Nan and I and baby Jean
There wasn't that much fun.

Cramped into a tiny room,
Ten bob a week the rent,
For years on end we tramped the streets
Our spirits nigh on spent.
Waiting for a council house
Through endless months and years.
Your Nana Jean, a nervous wreck
Shed many, many tears.
The day she washed the baby's clothes,
And hung them out in the summer sun
The landlady unpegged the lot,
And tossed them in our coal bin
You wouldn't call that fun.

The day your Nan aired the baby's clothes
On a line above the fire grate,
And all of them went up in flames,
How do we replace them, mate?
The time she went to Queen Street
To get milk coupons for our baby,
She'd not been gone too long,
When she returned unto the pram
She found our baby gone
Taken by some stupid mindless lady.

Can you imagine how she felt,
What went on in her mixed-up head
On looking in that empty pram
Amidst the public hue and cry?
Well that's real trauma my young friends
When you feel the world has reached its end,
And with it you should die.

As for me the road was rough
Keeping wife and child was tough.
Working all the hours God sent
To pay for food and clothes, and rent
Twelve hour shifts five days on end,
And Saturday morning shifts as well;
Falling asleep at home on my feet,
Harsh times, yes one could call it hell.
And as more children came along,
First two, then three, then four,
'Twas out at seven, and home at eleven
Before I entered our front door.
By which time, with kids in bed,
And Nan and me curled up by the fire
We'd sit and talk, and plan ahead,
Kiss good-night and wend our way to bed.

No TV, no radio,
Nor gramophone to call our own,
But there was music in our home,
The cries of babies many nights,
The din that came from children's fights,
The joy and laughter, tears as well,
That was our heaven,
That wasn't hell.

No hell is what you make it
When you always take not give,
And hell can be right here on earth
If you don't learn how to live.
If you're always finding fault
In the one you call your own,
If you nag or bitch, and want the world,
Then you should live alone.

When you're joined to one another
You must learn to give not take,
If you truly love each other
You must care only for your mate.
Caring for each other,
And sharing lows and highs
Is the love that drives dark clouds away,
And makes for sunnier skies.
Heaven on earth it well could be
Though the road may oft be rough,
If all the while true love prevails
When the going's really tough,
When it seems your boat has lost its sail,
And you feel you've had enough
That's when true love will guide the way
To a glorious Golden Wedding Day.

Ode to a Fag

Dear Martyn,

So glad to learn you're giving up smoking
Let me tell you a story, and I am not joking.
It begins when I was almost eighteen years old
Fit and strong, a soldier, World War Two was one week old.
I was youthful, brash and couldn't care less.
When I knocked on the door of the sergeants' mess
And asked for a packet of twenty 'Gold Flake'.
Band sergeant Joyce said 'Tom for God's sake
Don't start now', and he gave me a smack
Down three steps I fell, in a heap on my back.
As I looked up at him in a rage, and a lather
He threatened, and did tell the tale to my father,
Who, when I got home on my very first leave
Was as mad as hell, and not a little peeved,
And said 'Once you start another fag you will crave,
And before you know it son, you'll be a nicotine slave.'
It did not seem to do me any good,
For all my mates were smoking, and I felt I should.
What did it matter, for this was World War Two,
And we were 'cannon fodder', and all of us knew
That come the months and years ahead
Some of us would make it, and others would be dead.
That was the thoughts I had in my head,
Never knew that if I smoked I'd be just as blooming dead.

Nobody talked of cancers, or diseases obscene,
And almost every actor upon the 'silver screen'
Was puffing at a cigarette in almost every scene,
As though their life depended on the dreaded deadly weed,
And on this obnoxious habit, film buffs would nightly feed.
They'd see Bette Davies, 'Bogey' and Lauren Bacall,
And Crawford, and Cary Grant, and those I can't recall
Lighting up, and puffing in the smoke,
And they lit up their fags without a worry or a care,
And filled the cinema to the ceiling with rank and putrid air
That set them all a-spluttering, and coughing fit to choke.

The war went on for six long years,
And for the fighting soldier, a 'ciggy' held no fears.
If your comrade was hit, and death was close by
He would ask for a fag, before he could die.
It was always a fag, on which he would drag
As slowly his life ebbed away
And this bloody scene came up on the screen
In almost every war film that ever was seen
And there too were depicted the high society girls
With their evening dresses, pretty faces, peroxide hair in curls
In manicured fingers a 'ciggy' holder entwined,
Elegantly inhaling poisoned fumes of every kind.
A role model; a copy cat was the girl on leaving school
Who felt grown up, and all 'street wise'
Sharing fags and matches just like the guys.

Compared with wages, 'ciggys' were not that dear
And side effects were quite unknown, there wasn't much to fear
No warnings on the packet saying fags could mar your health,
And tobacco barons greedily stored up lots and lots of wealth.
There were 'Woodbines', 'Black Cat' and 'Four Aces', 'Craven A'
And there were 'Ardath' and 'Kensitas' and brand names I can't recall
And three 'Crayols' for a penny from dispensers on a wall.
That's how things were, when I was very young,
When puffing at a cigarette was regarded as great fun.
Not so funny, now that one's grown old,
Not clever at all, now everyone is told,
That smoking causes cancer of the lung,
Wish I'd known that when I was very young.
It also causes atheroma, and heart disease,
And clogs up all one's arteries.
Now at seventy-three, all these things have happened to me.
Two heart attacks, angina and coronary surgery,
And what does all that mean to a septuagenarian male
Who on the outside doesn't look so bad, but on the inside is quite frail.
Who cannot swim a yard or two without running out of puff
Who cannot walk just twenty yards, without saying 'That's enough,'

Who no longer digs his garden, but potters with a hoe,
And when he does it's stops and starts, and very, very slow.

So there it is my dear Grandson,
Smoking is not clever, smoking is not fun.
Why wait until you're old as me before the truth sinks in?
Parcel up your deadly fags, and throw them in the bin.
Save up all your money, and share it with your wife,
And I promise when you reach my age
You will enjoy a much more healthy life.

Hymn to the Holy Spirit

Come into our hearts, Holy Spirit
Increase our Love for you
Strengthen our Faith, Holy Spirit,
That we may always be true
True to our friends Holy Spirit,
Kind to all creatures in need
Come dwell in our hearts Holy Spirit
And plant in them your loving seed.

Come into our minds Holy Spirit
Show us the Holy Way
Light up life's path Holy Spirit
Guide us by night, and by day.
Hold fast our hands Holy Spirit
Firmly and never let go
We do need your help Holy Spirit
For good seeds in our minds to grow

Come into our souls Holy Spirit
Fill us with Grace and Peace.
Bring to us Joy, Holy Spirit
Let not our Love for you cease,
True to our Love Holy Spirit
We promise always to stay
Pure in our hearts and our minds, and souls
And to pray for your help every day.

The Mass is Ended

The Mass is ended, we go in peace,
Our hearts are carefree, our troubles eased.
Our steps are lighter, our voices sing
In praise of Jesus Lord, our God, our Christ, our King.

The Mass is ended, we go to spread
The words of Jesus, on which we've fed.
The Church, his People, who dine with him
Are one with Jesus Lord, our God, our Christ, our King.

The Mass is ended, we go to care
For those who need us, and with them share
The words of Jesus and with them win
A place with Jesus Lord, our God, our Christ, our King.

The Mass is ended, we go with love,
For one another, we set the dove
Of Peace and Friendship upon the wing
As did dear Jesus Lord, our God, our Christ, our King.

The Mass is ended, we pray for peace,
For all God's children to join the Feast,
And share the Good News, the news of him
Who died to save us, Jesus Lord, our Christ, our King.

The Mass is ended, with voices raised
To our Lord Jesus we all give praise
We promise truly to fight all sin,
And pledge our love to Jesus Lord, our Christ, our King.

To My Beloved On Our Golden Wedding Day

I don't reveal throughout the year the many thoughts within my mind,
That would imply that I'm austere, perhaps selfish, and unkind
I'd like to think this is not so, for I really try to do my best
Come wind or rain or hail or snow, I am content within our nest.

Having chosen from many others
A partner who is staunch, and true, who sticks in rough times just like glue,
Who cheers me up when all is doom, just being there dispels the gloom.
Who lights the way with spirit bright, who cares, and shares, and brings some light
To all the problems that arise, who mocks the dark clouds in the skies,
And when they're glowering down on me, threatening my peace and sanity
Brings bright clear light to saddened eyes, and sunlit blue and promising skies.

With you my love, I'm truly blessed, *Tempus Fugit* fleeting I fear,
It's time to say that you're the best, the one I hold most dear,
And it seems just right for me to say, on this our very special day
My Love for you grows deeper with each and every passing day.

Yesterday is Dead and Gone

1

Why does man get sorely troubled
Why so oft beset with woe,
Why can't each live for the other,
And make hate the common foe?
In this world where fearful conflict
Leads to grief, and dark despair,
Why can't each love one another,
And make laughter fill the air?

Refrain

Think on this my friends, and say
That yesterday was all so wrong
Think ahead, and build tomorrow
Yesterday is dead and gone.

2

An act of birth is all that claims us
Lending colour, race, or creed,
Why can't each see in the other
Simply humans of one breed?
We are children of but one God
Born to serve, and love, and care
To nourish those whose need is greatest
To give, and with them truly share.

Refrain

Think on this my friends, and say
That yesterday was all so wrong
Think ahead, and build tomorrow
Yesterday is dead and gone.

3

Why does man throughout his time span
Oft look backwards during life?
It's the past that flames the passions
Giving rise to fear, and strife.
Back in time, throughout the ages
Were sown the seeds that separate,
That fostered feudal power, and glory,
Engendered growth of greed, and hate.

Refrain

Think on this my friends, and say
That yesterday was all so wrong
Think ahead, and build tomorrow
Yesterday is dead and gone.

4

Now's the time for contemplation
Review the past, mistakes were there,
Let's learn from these, make reparation
Unite as one, the world to share.
Remember good times, be encouraged
By Faith, and Hope, and Charity,
And let historic evil perish
On rocks of new-found sanity.

Give us this Day our Daily Bread

1

I give you this day,
Do all things well.
I give you this day,
Do not dwell
On the 'morrow yet to come,
Nor the past now history,
I give you this day,
Do all things well for me.

2

I give you this day,
Do not lie abed.
I give you this day,
Rise to the work ahead,
Idle not, nor waste a moment
Of the time I give to thee,
I give you this day,
Do spend some time with me.

3

I give you this day,
Do aspire to grace.
I give you this day,
Turn not away your face,
For I am ever with thee,
In you I wish to abide,
I give you this day,
Pray, let me come inside.

4

I give you this day,
You asked for daily bread.
I give you this day,
Now I ask you to spread
The good news that I
Am always close by,
Not light years away
Like some star in the sky.

Know that is why
I give you this day.

War Games

A Twenty-First Century Fairy Tale, or is it?

He sat astride my bony knees
My great-grandson just seven
His eyes so innocent, light blue
A paler shade of heaven
Mischievously they sparkled
And with familiar inquiring gaze,
As ever he said 'Grandad
Talk to me of bygone days'.

I told him they were days of steam,
Of noisy smelly trains,
Of 'black diamonds' cut from Mother Earth
From deep within her veins.
He listened as I rambled on
Painting pictures of the past
All attentive, all agog
Then suddenly he asked,

'Tell me Grandad what was War?
So many friends have said
That nations fought each other
and didn't count their dead.
Must say that was a funny game
Killing people Gramps, what's more
It must have been a silly one
If they didn't count the score,
'Cos if they didn't count the cost
How did they know who'd won?
Did it matter, Gramp, who won, or lost,
Or did they fight for fun?'
'Well Tim,' I said, 'This game of war
That nations used to play
Had long gone on since time began
It's curious in a way.
For when the war game started
There wasn't much to fear,
The weapons then were primitive

A flint axe, or a spear,
Or maybe just a jagged stone,
Or a simple stabbing knife,
And enemies fought hand to hand
Taking one another's life.

And tribes were small in number
And tribes were very few,
So they could easily count the cost,
Every man that died they knew.
Later on with bows and arrows,
Stones flung by slings of leather
The warring tribes stood far apart
They wondered not, nor whether
The missiles leashed upon their foe
Had claimed a life. What's more
They left their own for carrion,
And they ceased to count the score.
That's the way it was; and then
Came sword and lance and gun,
Explosives were invented
Just adding to the fun,
And tribes became great nations,
And populations grew,
And somewhere in the wicked world
There sprang a war anew.

Very soon with smart invention
Came weapons of great size
Huge battleships upon the seas
And warplanes in the skies.
Massive tanks for land warfare,
Gases mustard and phosgene,
Splinter bombs and land-mines
All obnoxious, all obscene.
Now it wasn't just the armies
Who could play this frightful game
All women and the children
Were cannon fodder just the same.
They did not pull a trigger
Or release an aerial bomb,
But they counted in the scoring,

And it wasn't very long
Ere those non-combatant corpses
Outnumbered those who had to fight,
But they counted in the scoring
Mad warring nations took delight
In totting up the total
As though playing Bagatelle.
I tell you son, the war game
On our planet Earth was Hell.'

I paused to light my meershaum
Through the rising cloud of smog
Tim's eyes transfixed upon my face
Disbelieving, all agog
Twinkling as the stars at night
No signs of tiredness yet.
He said 'Grandad, you're joking
That's a fairy tale; I bet
If we could count all those who died
Through nations waging war,
Hell and Heaven could be jam-packed full,
Tell me Grandad, is there more?'

Puffing gently at my battered pipe
Quite lost in meditation
My thoughts collected carefully
I said, 'Well yes, there is son.
But let me tell you ere I start
This place called earth is Hell
Not somewhere horrid set apart
Mankind would do quite well
To remember this before they start
On a course of self-destruction
There'd be no Hell on Earth, nor Heaven
Just a great big void my son.
You see back in the twentieth century
Nigh on half-way through
There raged a war to end all wars,
They tagged it World War Two.
Many nations were in conflict
Throughout Europe to the East
And inflicted on each other

Great carnage, 'twas a feast,
Yet not enough to sate
The appetite of those who did not fight.
I mean those men who ordered scientists
To work through day and night
Those boffins took up the gauntlet
And laboured hard and long,
The offspring of their efforts
was the evil Atom Bomb

Dropped on Hiroshima and a place called Nagasaki
Causing horrid deaths and devastation,
They filled the peoples of this crazy world
With shock and trepidation.
From that time on there was great fear
Throughout the universe,
Despite all this, the scientists
Continued in research.
Then World War Two was over
The Atom bombs, its sad swan song
The repercussions of that day
Were to linger on and on.
For the victors and the vanquished
There was great sadness over all,
For the victors perhaps elation,
But over both there hung a pall,
The knowledge that mankind
In utter degradation
Had unleashed upon its simple self
This cursed and mad creation.

'What happened next then, Grandad?'
Said a weary tired Tim
As he dismounted from my knees
And cuddled close beneath my chin.
My arm around him folded
I held him warm against my breast,
And puffing feebly at my burnt out pipe,
I paused to take a rest.
And I reflected on that glorious day,
Did sanity prevail?
The day that all mankind found God,

The day that we now hail.
We know it as a holiday
It's called 'The Day of Peace'
I recall it as if yesterday
When wars just simply ceased.
No one here knows just what happened,
It was as though God cried, 'Now Halt,
Two thousand years I'd given you
And you still could find no fault
In slaughtering one another
As you prayed for peace, so fervently.
Well, the holocaust is over now,
You're here, in Heaven with me.'

I don't think Tim had heard me
Spin my yarn right to the end
He was sound asleep and snoring,
But you have read right through my friend,
And I pray to God in doing so
Your conscience has been stirred,
And made you see that you are Man,
Not just a unit of a herd
Prepared to follow those
Who conduct a symphony of hate
Stand up for Peace, be counted,
For all too soon 'twill be too late.

Heart-strings

Heart-strings once they were playthings,
Happy and gay things
Trembling and shaking,
And filled with a love I thought true.

Heart-strings; strings that you played on,
Never a note wrong,
Humming and strumming
And bursting with love just for you.

Heart-strings; vibrant only for you,
Heart-strings, tuned by a love I thought true,
Heart-strings, tortured and aching,
Tormented are breaking,
Tangled and twisted
Now filled with deep sorrow, and blue.

Heart-strings; strings that are numb now,
Strings that are dumb now,
Silent and lonely
And stilled till awakened anew.

Heart-strings; touched by a new love are playing,
New tunes or are they ghosts from the past?
Heart-strings; once more they are gay things,
Happy and carefree, caressed by a love that is new.

Heart-strings; tenderly played on,
Can it be so wrong,
Scheming and dreaming,
And praying that my heart rings true?

The Rose Bowl

If you for just one moment thought,
That for another this was bought,
Then darling one, you've not yet learned
In all these years how much you've earned
By simply being what you are,
The dearest, kindest wife by far.

This silver bowl with blooms inset
Is a present just for you my pet,
My wish is that you see each rose
As a token of a love that grows,
With each and every passing day,
My love unlike these roses
Will never fade away.

(Written to my wife who thought the Rose Bowl was a present for my sister Eileen)

If You Could Only Say

If you could only say I Love You,
If you would only say you care,
If you would only say I need you,
My life with you I'd gladly share.

I feel the passion of your kisses,
I feel the warmth of your embrace.
I see the lovelight in your eyes, dear
The blush of romance lights your face.

But you can't say the words I long to hear,
Three little words that lovers whisper
When they are near dear,
So close like this I feel your love is true
Yet my heart aches to hear you say
Darling I love You.

I whisper tenderly the words you want to hear,
You know I care, I bare my soul to you my dear,
I find it easy when you're near, to say,
How much I Love You.
Respondre, say you love me, *Parler moi d'amour*
Just whisper tenderly my darling, *Je t'adore*,
Please tell me, that you love me now,
I ask you dear for nothing more.

The Gentle Heart

Mother's Day dear Mum
Is a time for me to say
All the things I feel
That I don't tell you every day
To tell you what is in my heart
And how much that I love you
To thank you for your help
In the things you say and do,
To thank you for the gentle heart
That shares the aches of others
To thank you for clear-cut mind,
That unlike some other mothers
Does not burden those you love,
But takes the load and shares
All their problems, and who cares.
May you enjoy a happy Mother's day,
For it gives me this chance in my simple way
To say to you, and no other,
You are a very special Lady,
And to thank you for being my Mother.

On Becoming a Dad

There the little bundle of joy
Lay snug and warm beside his mum,
My eyes beheld my son, my boy,
A newborn babe, a life begun

And as I gazed in wondrous awe
Upon our child with mind awhirl,
With feet a metre off the floor,
In merry dance I did a twirl.

Then Jean, my wife, sat up in bed
And in voice becoming a Lady
All serene she coolly said
'Come down from there you'll wake the Baby.'

Gradually her voice grew loud
Her pleading fell upon deaf ears,
For I was higher than a cloud
My eyes in flood with joyous tears.

All through the din our Baby slept
Then I hugged and gently kissed my wife,
And out of the ward I merrily stepped
Aware that our son would change my life.

PS And he did

It was only a Dream

Buy a Television, a PC or a Video
With each one comes a little book
That tells you all you need to know
Such as how to switch them on and off,
And make the sound go high or low.

Buy a brand new motor car,
Or a second-hand old 'Banger',
And you'll never drop a clanger,
For in the glove compartment
When you have a look
You'll find another little book.

It tells you how to start the engine
And how to get each gear,
And very soon you're on the road
Without any kind of fear
You learn how to switch the main beams on,
And turn them off as well,
Next thing you're burning rubber
Like a mad Bat out of Hell.

Buy a marriage licence,
And say 'I Do', 'I Do',
Set out to build a love nest,
Just a little home for two.
Then you consummate your love,
And in it seems no time at all
You are three in number,
And you're climbing up the wall

For when our first-born came along
We had no book I'll have you know
To tell us how to switch him off,
Or turn the sound down low.
We knew just how to change a wheel,
And repair a tyre flat, but how to change a 'nappy',
Well, how do we do that?

Or what to do when baby's screams
Awoke us in the night,
How do we sort that one out,
For it often starts a fight,
And very soon the love nest,
Turns into a place called Hell
With no one at the ringside
To save us by the bell.

And then beside the bawling
The baby son is crawling.
All too soon he's on his feet,
And dashing here and there,
And soon our dream home, nice and neat,
Is turned into a real nightmare.
As he climbs upon the table
Via a handy dining chair,
And smashes all the china
That was nicely laid out there
Cups and saucers, plates go flying,
And sent crashing on the deck,
And Mam and Dad in desperation
Would like to wring his neck.

Soon, the toddling stage is over,
And the sprog is off to school.
The infant stage soon passes
And he's in the high school classes
Where it seems the teachers in despair
Are going nuts and tearing hair,
For now they're told they must not smack
A tearaway who's on the 'Crack'
Who smokes a fag or two as well,
And in general, raises merry hell.
Who mitches school with other boys,
And goes to town shops nicking toys.

'Twas then I woke up with a scream
All a tremble soaked with sweat
Then I realised 'twas all a dream,
And into the children's room I crept,
Just to have a little peep.
There they lay, four in number
Curled up warm, and fast asleep.

Lovely kids each one of them
I thought, as I crept back into my bed
And again I mused, how is it then
They're all as good as gold
Sharing with each other,
And caring for the old,
And always it appears to me
They do just as they are told.

So there we are, the story's told,
This tale comes to an end
With a lovely close-knit family,
And I tell you this my friend
When we started out together
We were clueless and naive,
And yet in spite of that
Both my wife and I believe,
That without a book to guide us
We managed without fuss
To bring up four delightful kids,
We trust and love so much,
And we both feel that all of them
Are very fond of us.

Spare the God, and Spoil the Child

I remember Christmas Day morning
A sock, not a stocking, filled with an orange,
An apple, some nuts, and a cracker,
And some bright pennies, that was just about all.
Maybe a box of tin soldiers, or a train set,
If Mam and Dad were flush,
Then downstairs I would rush
To find paper chains I'd helped to make,
Cascading from the ceiling, and draped around each wall.

No Christmas tree, no turkey,
Yet dinner was just fine
With Dad's pet Leghorns plucked and stuffed,
And carved, on which we'd dine,
And Mam who saved and slaved
To make the Christmas Cake and Pudding,
And dozens of Mince Pies
And seven kids with Mam and Dad
Stuffed ourselves unto the eyes.
Not caring what was yet to come
What food was left for Boxing Day
Eat, drink, and praise the Lord,
For this was Christmas Day.

The young man listened carefully
To all I had to say
His mouth agape in disbelief,
Then he had this to say.

'How times have changed these days
Who is this Lord you praised?
What was Christmas Day?
Something to do with a Babe in a Manger
I've heard some old folk say.'

'And what's all this about girls and boys
Having gifts of fruit and nuts, and toys?
Why man, I get fruit every day,
And as for toys with which I play
I only have to carp and moan
To make them come my way.'
Then he went on to say
'You can barely see the bed in my room
For all the things that I possess,
There by the window is my desk
On which my television rests,
And alongside it my computer lies
With video films and computer games
Stacked way up to the skies.
And there's my roller skates and my video
And my brand new personal stereo.
My dad bought me that yesterday
I only raved for one whole day,
And that is how it came my way.'

And I said to the young man
Who said his name was Ken,
'Don't you know the story
Of the Three Wise Men
Who followed a Star to Bethlehem,
That led them to a stable
Wherein Baby Jesus was born.
Don't you know that they brought gifts
Of Frankincense, and Myrrh and Gold,
And those three Kings paid homage
To a King not one day old.
Don't you know that it was Christmas Day
On a cold and frosty morn
When the little Baby Jesus
The King of Kings was born.'

The young man listened carefully
To all I had to say,
His mouth agape incredulously,
Then he had this to say; with I fear, a little sneer
'Oh! So that's why you celebrated Christmas
With lots of food and presents, and oodles of Good Cheer.'

And I said, 'Yes young man,
Our Christmas Day came only once a year,
And we kids got all excited
As the Festive Day drew near.
Now what young man excites you?
What have you got, to look forward to?
It seems to me that you have everything
That I think counts for nowt,
And all it seems you had to do,
Was to rant, and rave, and shout.'

Some thoughts on Nature

A very dear friend recently wrote the opening lines which gave rise to the following thoughts and words.

The needles have been blowing off the tall larch trees in the winds of the last few days in a sort of smoky golden rain. It has been so lovely in the bright sunlight.

Roses, hybrid and tea bravely strive to bloom on branches lashed by autumnal wind and rain; their petals threatening to explode into a galaxy of colour restrained now, wretched and forlorn; unaware that Mother Nature's heart is turning cold. Soon they will realise the battle can't be won, secateurs will trim them, but they will rise again to regale us in the summer sun.

Multifarious foliage, Goldenrod, Lavender, Phlox, Fuchias, Michaelmas daisies, once ablaze in colours of yellow, red and golden hue, with perfumes that pleasured the senses, now stand like petrified forests, shabby and forlorn awaiting the gardener's knife. They too in summer season will spring once more to life.

Another autumn full of colours that in youth we did not see;
A prelude to winter with blizzard, ice and snow
White landscapes beneath a mantle of dark skies cloister the aged,
Exhilarate the young of heart, their faces all aglow.
Do they, as we, see the magic of nature, or do the seasons pass them by?
Maybe so, although they know the joy of skating on iced waters, and sledging
In the winter snow; do they not see the tiny Snowdrops peeping at them from
The ground? Surely they must know they are the heralds of spring, a prelude to
Great hosts of Narcissus and Daffodil.

Do they not see the blossoming of trees, once naked and forlorn,
Bursting into life; each leaf newly born,
Maturing into foliage of every verdant hue
A certain sign that tells them summer time is almost due
With King Sol in majesty ablazing in the sky
Can it be true, that young folk do not espy
The sublime magic of each season passing by?
If this be true of those who pose,
How, What, Where, When, and Why,
Then we must teach the young
To view the grandeur of each season,
Through a pair of ancient eyes.

Words of Comfort

Think ahead dear Nell, and say
'All my tomorrows begin today'
Yesterday is dead and gone
Yet let sweet memories linger on.

Find pleasure Nell, in all you do
Seek to tread life's path anew,
Open doors which once shut tight,
Pass through and strive with all your might
To walk from darkness into light.

For you, dear Nell, have much to do,
Many are those who still need you,
And your strong faith will see you through.
With fondest love I truly say,
May joyful tomorrows begin today.

(To my dear sister following the death of her beloved husband Stan.

In the years that were to follow until she died in nineteen-ninety-five, she did indeed lead a very active and full life in spite of the fact that she constantly suffered with a heart problem. She was in and out of hospital; suffered valve replacement, warfarin regime, and almost weekly attendance at the cardiac clinic.

Despite all the trauma Nell became more and more involved in her parish church St Mary's Canton. She became a member of the New Theatre's Society of Friends; she joined the Town Women's Guild wherein she came to enjoy herself in the Choir. She also gave a considerable amount of her time to fund-raising for Guide Dogs for the Blind. An avid sports fan, she very much enjoyed cricket and tennis and became a member of the Glamorgan Cricket Club and a very lively and vociferous spectator at all home matches. Tennis was always her first love and her interest became increasingly intense year by year; Eastbourne and Wimbledon were almost her second homes and little holidays to both famous venues became a most enjoyable part of her life. Yes, I think it can be truly said that Nell came to enjoy the many years that were left to her following the loss of Stan, and I would like to think that in some small measure my beloved sister did in fact draw some strength from my words of comfort.)

Father Christmas Song

Jingle bells, Jingle bells
I've Jingled a long way
To come and see you children
From my homeland far away.

I live in a big castle, in a land of snow and ice
It's far away in Lapland, and it's very, very nice
It's dark all through the Winter
But I don't get the frights
'Cos in my Magical Castle
There are lots of fairy lights,
And I've got lots of Elves and Fairies
Making lots of Toys,
For me to bring on Christmas Eve
To all good Girls and Boys.

So be good Kids on Christmas Eve,
And close your sleepy eyes
Not a sound for me to hear
When I come down from the skies,
For I am always quiet, I don't make any noise
When bringing lots and lots of Toys
To all good Girls and Boys

Now I've got to go, back to Ice and Snow,
On my Sleigh, I'll make my way
With a big Ho-Ho-Ho-Ho.
Now all sing Hee-Hee-Hee,
And wave your hands on high,
Have a Merry Christmas Kids,
I Love you all – Good-bye.

When I Found You

When I found you, I found a Love so true,
Still get that thrill within when you are near,
So close my dear, or far apart, within my heart
I know that I will love you till I die
The love I've known like seed has grown
To blossom in the garden of my heart.

Your Love for me is like this melody,
Sweet haunting tune keeps fresh the bloom,
And passion's new
No spoken words convey the love I feel,
And so I pray, my song of Love
Will tell your heart that I Love you.

These lyrics were added to a clarinet solo written for, and entitled 'Acker'. Prior to the addition of the lyrics the music score was sent to the man who found fame with 'Stranger on the Shore'. In response his secretary replied to the effect that Acker's programme was full, and that the great man wrote for himself. It was to say the least a big disappointment, for I still feel that had my offer been taken up he might have found another 'Hit' for himself. One must live in hope, and I still feel that one day both the music and lyrics will be presented to the public. Wishful thinking! It may well be, but one must have faith in one's work. Somewhere out there in the world of popular music there must be a publisher who holds to my belief.

March: The Hall of Fame

We all, salute the names
Of famous sportsmen of our land.
Whose prowess, in their field
Enrolled them in this select band

With skill, and artistry
They won our praise and staked their claim
Their renown is enshrined
Forever in the Hall of Fame.

The march was composed, and accepted by the Hall of Fame committee and performed at the inauguration ceremony which took place in the National Sports Centre Sophia Gardens. Some time later the lyrics came to mind and it is now an ambition of mine to hear Band and Choir joined, in what I hope will be a stirring tribute to 'The Famous Sportsmen of Wales.'

The following lyrics were written by Clifton Horrell the former Musical Director of the Whitchurch Male Voice Choir, to whom I shall be forever grateful for his skilful Choral arrangement of my March.

Salute them now in song,
Salute them with a voice so clear,
Sing out proudly and strong,
Come fill 'The Hall of Fame' with cheer,

Let every voice give Praise,
Come now, Salute each Glorious Name.
Our voices now we raise,
Come let us fill 'The Hall of Fame'.

A Royal Suite

Composed within the year following the wedding of Prince Charles and Diana. How things have changed since then.

Synopsis

A forest glade, hunting horns, mead from the cask, roast from the spit. The Royal party in festive mood; wining and dining and dancing. The Prince joins in the festivity, he is not enamoured until (the Coda) when he falls in love at sight and in the repeat of the Trio sings the following,

'Prince Charming' Minuet

My eyes behold a maiden so fair,
A blue-eyed lass with long flowing hair.
She's tall, so slim, regal and serene,
I vow when I'm King, that she'll be my Queen.

There eyes meet, there is a change of mood, all are aware; the forest scents permeate the warm summer air. The vision of loveliness begins to dance, waltzing alone; cool, alluring, tempting. He is enticed and joins her in mood of great excitement; graceful and joyous. Their friends are drawn to the dance, the music wafts away, and melts into the placid evening air. Soon in the cool glade, warmed by the mead and dance, all are rested, amour abounds. The Prince, completely enchanted, woos his new love in song.

Romanza

I will always love you, I will always need you,
I have roamed this wide World
Seeking you my love and only you.
Now I've found you, my heart's all aglow,
Hold my hand, and never let it go
Let's share our lives together
You're the one who shared my dreams.

(Diana joins in duet with the Prince)

For I'll always love you, for you I will care,
And now that I've found you,
I have reasons to share, my life with you only,
My future with you,
My heart tells me truly
That I love only you.
I will always love you,
I will always need you.
Now that I have found you
I will never, ever let you go.
You have touched my heart, it's all aglow
Hold my hand, and never let it go,
We'll share our lives together,
We will always stay in love.

From the Heart

Synopsis

Item	Melody	Time in Minutes
1. Introduction	Spoken	½
2. The Catheter,	'Oh Susanna'	1½
3. In Limbo	'Beautiful Dreamer'	1
4. The Clinic	'Jeannie with the light brown hair'	1½
5. The Joint Consultation	Spoken	1½
6. On Going Home	'Camptown Races'	2
7. On Being Home	'Poor Old Joe'	2

(All melodies are those of the American Composer Stephen Foster (Died 1864) Copyright is therefore valid no more, but apologies just the same.)

Introduction

To all who strived and strained
To alleviate our pain,
To the nurses who all worked willingly,
To the doctors on the ward
Who with miserly reward
Made sure that we progressed, steadily.

This I give to you
A patient's eye view
As my simple way of saying - Ta,
To everyone of you
From the Op theatre crew
To the ladies who brought me my - char.

Oh Catheter

Melody - 'Oh Susanna'

So – I went into the 'Heath' one day
'Twas a Thursday in the spring.
After taking blood, and a chest X-Ray,
A staff nurse filled me in

OH, CATHETER,
The thought makes my hair curl,
We are going to meet tomorrow
And my head is in a whirl.

So, a doctor chap came sat by me
He could see I was uptight
And he said 'This job tomorrow friend
Is going to be alright.
For this catheter, is a job we do quite well
And the video film that we do take
Helps the surgeon to excel.'

So – I had a bath on the Friday morn,
'Sweeny Todd' had left me bare
And they wrapped me up in a nice white gown
With a pill I did not care.

OH, CATHETER
It was over I was glad
With all so kind, I did not mind,
And the TV weren't too bad.

In my groin, they stuck a large sandbag
I swear it weighed a ton,
For twelve long hours I just lay there,
And it paralysed my bum.

GOODBYE CATHETER
Saturday morning, I was gone
They said that they would send for me,
And the wait won't be too long.

In Limbo

Melody 'Beautiful Dreamer'

I waited and waited, and time drifted by,
Weeks turned to months, and I wondered why,
No-one had written, asking for me
To see the surgeon; alas woe is me.

Gone and forgotten, neglected poor thing,
Wife said 'I'm fed up, I'll give them a ring.'

No - wait for the Clinic, it's sometime in June.
And maybe with some luck, they'll send for me soon.

The Clinic

Melody 'Jeannie with the light brown hair'

My wife's named Jeannie, with highlights in her hair
A little tint of colour - to hide the grey that's there.
She's lucky that she has not gone white like virgin snow,
No thanks to Medical Records, and the fright they gave her so.

When at the Cardiac Clinic,
The doctor said to me
'It's you that lives – 4, Angle Place
You are named Tom Kelly,'
I answered 'True', and said, 'Now Doc what's going on?'

He said 'They've gone and writ you off
Although you ain't been dead too long.'
I said, 'Now in this state, what can you do for me?'
He smiled, and promised truly, Mr Butchart soon I'd see.

The Joint Consultation

I saw Mr Butchart, Mike Stephens too was there
In a joint consultation, they said, 'Please take a chair,
We are very glad to see you,' both together said,
'And it's our considered opinion, now we know that you're not dead
That we can dramatically improve the quality of life,
By undergoing surgery.'

Here they turned unto my wife
And said 'He will be able to go swimming, and revel in L'Amour.'
Jean replied ''Twill be a miracle, 'cos he couldn't do those things before.'

'AHEM!' From Mr Butchart,
'In all modesty I say,
The miracles we perform at once
The impossible may take us a day

Therefore do not be surprised
For when we do this by-pass
Before your very eyes,
He will seem to get brighter,
At least – after the venal graft,
His troubles, we hope will be lighter,
And you'll find him not quite so daft.'

Before I could agree
To having surgery
My wife chipped in,
And coolly uttered with a grin,
'If all the things you say
Come to pass - then make the day
As soon as poss.
Do hurry up, and fit him in.'

And oblige her they did
With little hesitation,
For on July the twenty-fifth,
I had the operation.

On Going Home

Melody 'Camptown Races.'

I was sat down on the toilet, when
A Staff Nurse hollered me,
'Get your bum right off that seat, my lad
Mr Keenan's here to see
If you are fit and well,
If you're firing on all four,
'Cos if you are, you're out my lad,
And your feet won't touch the floor.'

'If you're firing on all four-Ha-Ha,
Then your feet won't touch the floor,
'Cos the cardiac mob
Have done their job,
And it's that way to the door.'

And so it came to pass my friends
I was given the big OK.

It was zero plus just ten days,
And I'd made it quick they say.
Nurse whipped the stitches out,
Then she saw my upper calf
'You'll not be going home today,'
And there came an echoing laugh.

Ain't going home today – Ha Ha,
Ain't going home today,
When your leg's alright
You'll be on your bike
But you ain't going home today.

'Twas the following day, on the Friday morn,
When she peeped beneath my gown,
From a height, I swear of five feet ten
Those bright eyes twinkling brown,
Surveyed my upper scar,
And she then said 'There you are
In just one day everything's OK.
You'll be going home by car.'

Going home by car – Ha-Ha,
'Cos you don't live very far,
I have phoned your wife,
You have plagued my life,
You'll be gone by two – Hurrah.

On Being Home

Melody 'Poor old Joe'

Gone are the days
When to walk was to invite,
Stops and starts, and pains,
And lashings of 'Tri-Nite'
Now, up a hill
With the wind keen in my face,
'Twould take the whole brigade of Guards
To halt my pace.

Gone are the days
When my head was bended low,

Gone are the days
When my heart was fraught with woe,
Gone are the times,
When Angina ruled my life,
Thank God for Eric Butchart,
And his magic knife.

Within the month following discharge from hospital, the words were conjured up; as previously said to the music of Stephen Foster. Together with son-in-law, Howard Morgan, on guitar, and his friend, Hugh Thomas on keyboard, and yours truly giving voice, an audio tape was produced, and presented to cardiac surgeon Eric Butchart. It was received with pleasure and some amusement, and it is the expressed hope that it will help to relieve a great deal of anxiety from anyone who has the misfortune to undergo heart surgery.

Without a shadow of doubt it made a great impact on my wife Jean, who in 1992 underwent a quadruple by-pass heart operation. She faced the ordeal with great fortitude, and made a quite remarkable swift recovery.

This family owes more than a great deal to those magnificent, dedicated people who devote most of lives to saving lives, and is deeply in their debt; some debts can never be repaid.

The Dentist's Chair

Something I just had to say
A tribute in lines *Vers Libre*
If you chuckle with mirth
My attempt at 'Free Verse'
Will be worth all my effort today.

And perhaps when you're old and you're grey
Just a bit like I am today
You will look through these pages
Go back through the ages
And recall that 'One fine day in May'.

When so young at the 'Heath'
Busy pulling old teeth
Your bad luck found me there in your chair
With roots two foot long, and all going wrong,
You damn nigh lost all of your hair.

So, in light-hearted mood
Hope you'll not think me rude
So blatantly facetious, and merry
I say thank you to you, and all of your crew
With a bottle of Harvey's Cream Sherry.

'Twas Thursday 26th of May, in nineteen-eighty-three,
An appointment was made for a.m. time, precisely nine-thirty.
It was around about ten
When they called me, and then
Sat me down in a modern dental chair
As I settled my behind
I thought of 'Mastermind'
All felt cosy, and truly set fair.

Under my tongue, I placed a 'Tri-Nite'.
The dentist chap adjusted the light
To shine on the molar, well filled, and infected
Well, that's what the clever X-Ray had detected.
It was then the first needle was jabbed in my gum,
And I thought when this happened four times again
That maybe one big jab, right into my bum,
Would suffice to short circuit all kinds of pain.

'Twas then that the ruddy drama began
The pliers, gripped firmly, by the young man,
Were clenched to the molar, undoubtedly diseased,
And he gently tugged, and he gently eased
The tooth this way, then that – then tugging a hellish lot more,
I was sure that the roots went right through to the floor.

There followed ten minutes of swift cut and thrust
As he duelled with the tooth, then gasped out 'I must
Rest for a while, 'ere my right arm falls off.'
He said 'I'll change the pliers.' I emitted a nervous cough.
Now freshly armed, let battle recommence
Reinforcement arrived in the shape of a wench,
Who happened to be a dentist, and so
Her hand I held tightly – and never let go.
Such a lovely, kind-hearted comforting girl
Was it she or the trauma that made my head whirl?
For by now I felt giddy, it seemed like two years
That I'd been sat in that chair, and then my worst fears
Were realised, as the tooth, broke off with a crack,
And the pliers crashed into top teeth with a smack.

'We'll rest for a while', said the brave-hearted one
And, after a breather, plunged into my gum
With a probe, and strong pair of tweezers to boot,
He fiddled, and prodded, and came out with a root.
I sighed with relief, and thought, 'Well that's done,'
He whispered to me, 'There is just another one'.

Again with probe and tweezers exploring the cavity
The expert hands did their job, by now it seemed to me,
I'd spent a lifetime in that chair,
This can't be real, this is not fair
For only last week, they took a wisdom tooth out
No fuss, no bother, and nowt to shout about.
Just as I was thinking thus, feeling wan and white,
In tweezers firmly grasped, the second root came into sight.

I knew then that my ordeal was completely o'er
It had lasted for an hour, perhaps a little more,
The young man's eyes showed great relief,
My God! that was bloody hard work,
He had chosen his profession, extracting humans' teeth,
And not for one moment did he shirk
The problems, as fast each came his way,
He met them head on, and with great expertise
Overcame all, and kept me at ease.
And I thought as I sat recovering there
This man is of a special kind of breed,
The sort that we, when in pain, and despair
Can turn to, in our desperate need.

And I also thought of those who rant, and rage
In constant avid pursuit of superfluous wage.
How much would they measure, in terms of fair play
Such a man whose dedicated task, day by day
Is, as he sees it himself, to rid humans of pain?
Well the answer to me is quite simple and plain.
All the gold, and silver in this world could not pay
For the arduous hour spent, treating me, that day in May.

Vintage Years?

Boyhood days on the Mynachdy Council Estate added up to Vintage Years, but not for Mums with big families, and Dads without gainful employment. Hit by the 1926 General Strike, and devastated throughout the impoverished 'Thirties'; how they managed and survived, God only knows. To a great extent they did so by caring and sharing; a rub of a neighbour's soap, a lend of a cup of sugar, a borrowed half-a-crown until Friday. 'Plural Family' might aptly describe the integrated unity of such a community, for no single family unit could afford to live in isolation. In general, poverty was the catalyst that cemented the neighbourhood bond of friendship, wherein envy and greed were truly conspicuous by their absence.

Children were not oblivious to their parents' stressful and traumatic daily routine; and more often then not, the older kids came to regard themselves as appendages to their parents' adult world, rather than children in the accepted sense of the word. It followed that such kids leading the pecking order soon found themselves involved in the financial gymnastics of family economics, becoming in the process what many would label as 'Street Wise'.

It wasn't that; it was simply an early desire to become an inherent part of their parents' daily struggle. Dad's chickens – Sussex, Leghorns, and Rhode Island Reds – laid many fine eggs; many of which, along with bouquets of mint from his garden were vendible products that for a few coppers, found their way into the more affluent homes of society. Miles of tramping to the far-flung high-class residential areas were for meagre financial returns that in all probability would not meet the cost of having a kid's pair of shoes cobbled.

Up at dawn to assist the local milkman as he wended his way with horse and cart. No milk bottles then; no 'Gold Top' nor 'Silver Top', just plain ordinary nourishing milk scooped from the clanging banging milk churns. Long drawn out treks; plenty of hurrying and scurrying; more worn-out shoe leather, all brought to a halt by a different clanging, the sound of school bells. Another half-a-crown at the week's end to pour into the family coffers.

Co-op broken biscuits in a big blue bag for sixpence, cracked eggs from the 'Maypole' shop, fairly cheap. Misshapen loaves, half price, and late on a Saturday night in addition to the princely sum of another half-a-crown, a large bag of damaged fruit from Joe Pope the Greengrocer for errand boy services rendered. What did Mam call them? Ah yes, 'bruised fruit', a quarter the price of unblemished produce. Oh yes, Mam could teach the Chancellor of the Exchequer how to balance a budget. In such a climate one still regards times of childhood and growing up as vintage years.

Potato or Tate and Lyle sugar sacks and some beanstalks nicked from someone's allotment made tents that Geronimo would have been proud of. He smoked his pipe of peace and maybe hallucinated; the lads smoked old dried up fern rolled up in *South Wales Echo* paper; any hallucinations they may have experienced were quickly short-circuited by bouts of sickness, and exploding fits of coughing. Swimming in the canal in the 'buff' alongside derelict barges, amidst a clutter of anything from floating dead dogs to sunken bicycle wheels, discarded tyres, and broken bottles. This was a luxury only to be outdone by very late illegal sorties over the perimeter fencing, and into the chlorinated healthier water of the Llandaff Fields open air swimming pool.

Childhood was a time of adventure, on safari with air-rifles, hunting rats along the banks of the river Taff, and fishing for 'tadders' in the Lock Field stream. Playing Tarzan high in the 'Yankee' Wood trees and Robin Hood in the brush. Peashooters made from the canes that abounded there, and bird nesting, a more leisurely pursuit. There were a conglomerate of outdoor activities that burned up youthful energy, and diminished the urge, not too prevalent at the time, to participate in unlawful activities.

Don't be misled, the boys had knives; nearly every boy had a pocket knife for Christmas. This was a very useful implement with which one could manufacture bows and arrows and yokes for slings, and make boats to sail on Roath Park Lake, and even sharpen a pencil or scrape a carrot purloined from a neighbour's garden. Somehow they never found a need to stab anyone; nor was it the done thing to kick someone into a state of hospitalisation, or mug and rob defenceless old folk.

Differences of opinion to extensive degree were invariably settled down the lane, where in the manner of latter day duellists, the antagonists would honourably resolve their problem toe to toe; with a 'bunch of fives' here and a 'knuckle sandwich' there, huffing and puffing; a flurry and a scurry, no skill whatsoever, unless it was one's misfortune to encounter a virtuoso pugilist from the Cathays, or Philog Boxing Clubs.

Such bouts of physical jousting more often than not ceased with no more than a bloodied nose, or a shiner. The latter was often looked upon as a badge of honour as in the days to follow the contusion mellowed to nothing more than a sepia-coloured stain, and again, more often than not the participants, set on bashing the living daylights out of one another, became or remained friends. Come to think of it I had seven black eyes, counting among them the monstrous one obtained when a pseudo medicine ball, conjured up from an iron dumbbell shrouded in wrappings of *Echo* paper encased inside an extremely worn out football case, and hurled by a Goliath of a senior scout escaped my pair of diminutive 'cub' sized hands, and landed dumb-bell side on my left eye.

Does a depressed economic climate, and accompanying depravation escalate criminal activity? That seems to be the thoughts abroad at this time. Could it perhaps be true in those far-off vintage years if 'scrumping' apples is taken into account? This was a delightful challenging adventurous escapade guaranteed to create a thrill and jangle the nerves of the youthful miscreants, especially when the alarmed shout of 'Cave' went up and the farmer gave chase.

The trick then was to scamper like bats out of hell, each in a different direction. This was very confusing for the outraged pursuants, and highly educational for the scampering horde as the night air became polluted, and gravely disturbed by expletives quite alien to the language taught in their schools. Funny too when some wag would shout, 'But I have got a Mam and Dad!'

Shanks's mare, or shanks's pony, that was our transport; one's own legs carried their owner for miles and miles. A Sunday evening stroll with the 'Gang' would circumnavigate all of Cardiff taking in Llandaff; Grangetown; over the Duke of Clarence bridge, up through James Street, Bute Street (The Old Tiger Bay), through the Town. (We called it town although it was a 'City' yet to become the Capital City.) On via St Mary Street, up the old canal bank, into the 'Lock' fields, over the railway lines, and back to the happy old stamping ground tired and ready for bed.

No mountain bikes then, but with consummate ease most youngsters could straddle a leg 'twixt the frame of Dad's bike, and thrill to the twisting, leaning experience of pedal power. Invariably such freedom of movement led to a breed of young artisans bent upon engineering their own transport. To this end frames, handlebars, wheels and chains were scrounged from Tips and Scrap Yards, and with great ingenuity many a 'Heath Robinson' mode of personal transport was created. Did it matter that wheel diameters differentiated twenty-four or twenty-six inch; that the rusty old chains disengaged from the cogs?

Not one iota, well not until a speedy descent down Llantarnam Road hill deposited the intrepid rider into someone's garden hedge and down that same hill many a self-constructed 'bogie', failing to take a bend, came to meet the same fate.

No computers then, nor television, therefore, in the modern idiom, no 'Couch Potatoes', but wireless sets began to find their way into the homes of those who could afford them. These were generally acquired on the never-never plan for a few 'bob' a week.

From the Savoy Hotel in London, the BBC made its very first daily broadcast on 11 November 1922; the writer was then just a year and ten days old. A decade later the British Broadcasting Company became a Corporation and moved to the magnificent Broadcasting House to broadcast daily programmes under national and regional banners.

Such a miracle of the age came to inspire the youthful bicycle engineers and their desire to become clones of Isambard Kingdom Brunel subsided as they endeavoured to emulate the great physical Guglielmo Marconi by Building 'Crystal Sets'; their very own personal wireless detectors. Another interest, another challenge; a pastime and a hands-on hobby guaranteed not to turn the aspiring electronic engineers into couch potatoes. If the youthful busy bees were not manufacturing bikes or wireless sets, or involved with fretwork saws, or Meccano sets then outdoors was the place to be. Out in the open air; an alfresco life away from the siblings, running free to meet the call of the wild. Rounders on the Green; the sound of broken glass; a whip round of hard-earned pocket money to repair the damage. Releaster, Bombarino, Hop-scotch, Rat-Tat-Ginger, and a host of other games clouded in the mist of time; all brought to an end by a variety of parental voices in cacophonous chorus bellowing 'Get in here, it's bedtime.'

Further education took place in the Gabalfa lending library wherein one could browse and study to one's heart's content. Budding masters of the 'Green Baize' game could lose their pocket money in no time at all to the wandering 'sharks', the con artists who invaded the Regal billiard hall. Both leisure institutions were swallowed up by the construction of the North Road roundabout, as was much later the Plaza Cinema, wherein, on a Saturday, literally hundreds of kids in the 'Tuppenny' rush could escape into the magic world of Hollywood.

Inside the palatial cosy comfort of that wonderful house of entertainment they found such idols as Johnny Weismuller and Errol Flynn, role models for those adventures in the 'Yankee Woods', and the gentle breast- and side-strokes of the canal water babies gave way to the magnificent Weismuller's 'American Crawl'; not an apt term for a new technique that permitted the lads to cut through the water at a fair rate of knots as though pursued by a crocodile.

As for high days and holidays, great jollification abounded annually on May Day as Mams and Dads and all the kids revelled in the 'Carnival'.

The old Mynachdy Institute was the anchor, and from there gaily decorated floats; carts with dancing girls and children in fancy dress paraded and all set out in gay abandon touring the estate to rapturous applause that echoes down the years to this day. And well remembered to this day is that first celebration, when in a special float garlanded with multifarious flowers and escorted by a bevy of gaily dressed girls, there rode in majesty Mynachdy's first May Queen, Susie Woods, a teenager of immense beauty who captured the hearts of everyone, not least among them the pseudo Tarzans and Robin Hoods of the period.

That was the high day; the high fortnight came with the Fun-Fair; owned by someone named White or Danton if rightly remembered. A huge conglomerate of chair-o-planes, swings, roundabouts and side stalls were sited and erected in next to no time on land adjacent to what was once called the Orbital Road, now the Western Avenue. The noise, the multicoloured lights, the sight and smell of the traction engines; the caravans; the hustle and bustle of the crowds, the raucous bellowing voices of the Barkers; the crack of rifles and the little faces clouded in candy-floss still linger in the memory. There wasn't much homework done around that time, in fact not a lot of anything was done for the site was a magnet to young and old.

For the lads, the super magnet was the boxing booth. Up on the platform in front of the 'Ring' stood the promoter with a voice like a town crier challenging all red-blooded males to 'Go three rounds' with any of his four or five bruisers. There they stood, gloved ready for combat, towel over shoulders, arms akimbo, glowering down; battle-scarred ugly brutes. They made Frankenstein's Monster look like Shirley Temple, and sent shivers down the spine. They did mine, but they did not deter a gladiator in our tribe, one who, if the memory doesn't play tricks, was named Sammy Bailey. Sammy took up the challenge, did himself proud, fought a good fight, went three rounds, and pocketed his purse and forever after bathed in the limelight of our hero-worship.

Today a number of sons and/or daughters still reside in the Mynachdy homes of their parents. Hope is expressed that they will have enjoyed this trip down memory lane; a journey back through time that recalls those halcyon days of childhood in a caring, sharing society.

'A phrase of melancholia due to the unsatisfied desire to return home'; that is how a certain dictionary describes nostalgia. In another we find it to be 'A sorrowful longing for conditions of a past age'. To the writer the latter seems to be a rather more profound connotation, but only in terms of childhood memories, already described as 'Vintage Years'. It is very doubtful that in maturity, parents of that era would have 'longed for conditions of a past age'.

On Your Silver Wedding

Twenty-five years close together
Through times mostly good rarely bad
Of these we've known each other twenty,
So I'm entitled to pay tribute to you, Jim and Glad.
There comes on a great day like this
A rare opportunity to say
What is held in the heart constantly,
What one deeply feels every day,
That we live our lives just the one time
Meeting pals, buddies, mates on the way,
But Friends, Real Friends, True Friends,
Are as rare as full moonlight by day.

Now I count among God's holy blessings
My good fortune, having friends such as you
Who've spent all these years giving, sharing
With no fuss, no bother, and no ballyhoo
So thanks to you both, I am proud
Of the past that I've shared with you two
As you look to the future together
May the skies above always be blue,
May you reap the rewards of your giving,
May your hearts always be young and gay,
Above all, may you both be together
When we celebrate your great Golden Day.

Ode to a Marathon Blow

It was Saturday October 18th in nineteen-eighty-two,
St Alban's Band went on the field
'Twas just gone half-past two.
The Band was not too large that day,
It only numbered twenty-two.
Off they went with a stirring march,
By chance called 'Sons of the Brave'
They weren't to know by kick-off time
Each would have worked like a slave.

Three o'clock was fast approaching,
Alun Priday switched on to say
The kick-off time would be delayed
Coventry's bus had broke down on the way.
They were stuck in a place just outside Usk,
And in order to save the day,
Cardiff had sent an omnibus,
Which also broke down – 'Sad to say'.

Meanwhile the valiant Band played on,
Through March, and Waltz, and Blues.
Not one carp or a single moan,
As they played, and awaited some news.
It came from Alun, the Cardiff Sec,
Who informed the dwindling throng
A fleet of cars led by 'Tony the Chair'
Had set off, and it wouldn't be long
Ere they returned with the Coventry side,
So for God's sake chaps hang on,
For if you don't, there will be so few of you,
You'll surely be outnumbered by our Band of twenty-two.

Meanwhile the valiant Band played on,
Knowing now they were into a fight,
The Club house clock showed ten-past four
As they played 'All through the Night'
Billy Kelleher their Honourable Sec,
To be in London took flight
He packed his 'Eupho' picked up Sue,
Foot down on the gas and up the M4 flew.
He had better luck than 'Tony the Chair',
For his brand-new car got him safely there,
And with Susie; his delightful, delicious mate,
Arrived in London at twenty to eight.

The voice of Alun, once again,
As five o'clock drew near,
Announced in tones of great relief,
That raised a hearty cheer.
'Good News, the Coventry team's arrived
The match will start at a quarter past five.'
By this time it's sad to say,
A lot of folk had gone away,
A loss to Band, and Club; not funny,
Of supportive staff of life called money.
Which prompts a prudent thought
Of great profundity;
No amount of copper, nor silver, or gold,
Can replace the bond of loyalty,
That is sixty-three years old.

Meanwhile the valiant Band played on,
What a baptism for Deputy Leo,
'John the Baton' had gone on holiday that morn,
And we ask ourselves; 'What did he know?'
As he dined, as he swam, as he danced through the day,
Had he slightly diverted his route on the way
And nobbled the coach with the Coventry team,
So that somewhere near Usk it ran out of steam?

You may ask 'my dear Watson'; Why did he do this?
I'll tell you dear folk, the Band needs the practice,
For next Sunday week it's up with the lark,
To be at a venue not far from 'Arms Park',
And they have to start playing at just after eight,
At the start of the Marathon, and I'll tell you this mate,
He may not be here, but on hols far away.
It's him who made sure we played nearly all day,
Who sorted out music, we did not repeat,
And made sure of enough, to perform such a feat.
So for me it's no longer a dark mystery,
The 'Marathon Blow' was set up cleverly
By the silver-haired gent, with cherubic face,
Who made absolutely certain, he'd be nowhere near the place.

Dawn Awakening

Alarm a-ringing challenging, bidding awake you poor mortal
King Sol, his crimson crown just glowing
Has changed to grey the darkness of the night
Roosters long have crowed, and failed to break
The embrace of Morpheus, clasping, gripping tight.
Feathered friends already on the wing,
Their fluffy nestled offspring chirping with delight:
The milkman's rattled and chinked upon his way,
And long passed out of sight.
The aged Mortal lies undisturbed, and unaware
As the grey of drawn gives way to morning light.
Peaceful and serene, the mortal remains are still
Oblivious to the voice of dawn, the soul has taken flight.

Postscript

Knock that knocker, ring that bell,
Say 'How are you, are you well?'
'Anything I can do for you to-day?'
You'll feel so much better when you walk away.

The Tattoo

When I was young, so very young
Just eighteen years of age
I was just a fledgling actor
Upon this worldly stage.
My parents whom I'd left behind
Were always loving, and so kind
Producers and Directors,
Each taught me to be refined.

They guided me for eighteen years
They spoke of me with pride,
I never thought I'd bring them tears,
Or take them for a ride,
But there came the day I left the nest
And went off to fight the War,
I suppose they thought, we've done our best
He's grown-up now, not raw.

But little did they know how much
I needed them each day
To counsel and advise me
As I went my own sweet way.
I was a fighting soldier strong,
I'd stand or fall alone,
I needed nobody's advice
All decisions were my own.

Well, that's the way it was
In bombed London nineteen-forty,
There was Norman, Jack and me
Big-headed, free and haughty
Walking down this sleazy street
We saw this shady shop,
It was a tattoo artist's place
Which brought us to a stop.

Norman said ‘I’ll have a tattoo
A loving heart upon my arm,’
Jack said ‘I think I’ll have one too
It can’t do any harm.’
So in we went, the three of us,
And Norman brash and bold
Had a great big heart with arrow through.
And loving words enscrolled.

He was newly married, and so
His love was to his wife,
I wondered if it lasted
’Cos her name was there for life.
Then Jack sat down to have his done,
The same sort of stupid thing,
He’d got engaged on his last leave,
And bought his Jill a ring.

The next time he went home on leave
To see his see his sweetheart Jill,
He came back very sad, and peeved,
In fact he was quite ill.
He’d shown to her his love token
Upon his arm laid bare,
She laughed at him, and said,
‘You’re mad, for someone else I care.

‘I’ve fallen for another guy
A pilot in the RAF.
He’s smart and clever, not like you,
You must be bloody daft.’
I’ve often thought of Geordie Jack
Searching the rest of his life
For a likely lass, with the name of Jill
Who he could make his wife.

My story's not yet reached the end
I had no girl, I was quite free.
Jack and Norman said 'No guts Welsh friend.'
I said 'You'll bloody see.'
Then I sat down to have the RA badge
Transcribed upon my arm,
I thought it better than a heart,
Can't do a lot of harm.

Little did I see that day
Just how much harm I'd done.
It might have been a wiser move
Had he tattooed my bum.
For when I went home both parents
Very quickly spotted it.
Mam simply cried, and Dad gave me
A lot of verbal stick.

He was as mad as Hell, and said
'You'll rue the day you had that done.'
How right he was dear grandson,
Because it hasn't been much fun.
It was alright in the army
And when I worked on factory floor,
But when I got promotion,
The fun flew out the door.

Sat in the manager's office,
Or in meetings upper class,
With shirt sleeves down I felt a clown,
'Cos somebody would ask,
'Why don't you roll your sleeves up
It's awfully hot in here?'
I always said, 'No, it's quite alright.'
For inside there was great fear.

What would my colleagues think of me
Well-educated, and refined?
Who would mutilate his body?
He must have a tiny mind.
So there it is dear grandson,
Every word I swear is true
I wish I'd known a grandad
Who loves me, like I love you.

You see my son the scars you bear
Since you were very small
Caused all of us great heartache,
And we so well recall
That Sunday, when the teapot
Came down from off the shelf
It was an accident you know,
Not wounds inflicted by yourself.

So, ponder well on all I say,
Stay unblemished, and feel clean,
For I have always rued the day
I got tattooed when eighteen.

Diana, Queen of Hearts 1961–1997

How sweet the name Diana
Roman Goddess of the Moon,
She who brought Light;
Synonymous with Artemis
Greek Goddess of Mother Earth

How sweet the name Diana,
Goddess of the Modern World,
Patroness of Charity,
Soulmate of Humanity,
Goddess of Mother Earth.

How sweet the name Diana,
Daughter of Aristocracy
Mother of Royal Princes,
Sister of the *hoi polloi*
Goddess of Mother Earth.

How sweet the name Diana,
How truly sweet the name,
That forever will remain
Upon the lips of all mankind
Princess of Mother Earth.

How sweet the name Diana,
Royal Princess of Wales,
Destined never to be Queen,
Yet Queen of Hearts, o'er all the World
Forever she will reign.

To All Who Are Estranged

You grew up as a family; sharing toys,
Your clothes, your joys.
You also shared your sorrows,
Your common blood did boil
When so young, a sister and brother
Left this mortal coil.
You joined in unison to ask,
'Why did they have to die?'

That was a time of unity,
A family with one voice,
When each could feel the other's pain,
When a shoulder was there to cry on,
And a hug to let each know
The feelings deep inside.
And as the darkened clouded skies
Gave way to sunny happier times,
You as one big family
Knew just how to rejoice.

Whatever happened, one might ask,
As the years have swept so swiftly by,
To the kids who learned to love and care,
Oh yes, we all find reasons why.
Can there be a single one
That causes love to die?

Man's life span is so fleeting,
Gone in the blink of an eye,
Why wait until the end is nigh,
Why wait until the time we die
Ere we say ''Twas never meant
That we should live our lives apart'
And with an agonising cry,
Say, 'I'm Sorry Love, Goodbye'.

The day after writing this, I read the following words in our parish magazine: 'Death can leave a lot of unfinished business: words of forgiveness never spoken, love never communicated, business matters incomplete, work never done.'

A Loser

Written on hearing the famous film actor and racing car enthusiast Paul Newman say 'Show me a good loser, and I'll show you a Loser.'

On seeing the averages last season
And finding that I was last but one,
I decided next season to play hard to win
And not muck about, and have fun.

You don't see a fighter shake hands, and say
'Jolly good luck, do have fun.'
No he'll squint at the guy, and with hate in one eye,
Say 'You'll be flat on your back in round one.'

You do not see a 'Prop', gently pack down
Whispering sweetly 'Please don't rip my kit.'
No he grapples and grunts, grabs the 'Hookers' right ball
And squeezes the 'Tight Heads' left tit.

So the moral is clear, you're bowling to win
With a bowl in his hand, and his eye on the Jack
To nobble the Prat's just the thing. Look him straight in the eye
And say with a sigh 'You stepped off the mat, that's a sin.'

Then chatter and natter and kick bowls about
Distract Prat's attention, tell the Skip with a shout,
'The bowl that's just ended alongside the Jack
Is illegal, the Prat had his foot off the mat.'

I've always been taught, that to be a good sport
Is how one should approach every game,
But I've given much thought to the battles I've fought
And lost with my head bowed in shame.

So, it's good-bye to the 'Have a good game'.
And farewell to the handshake's 'Well done',
If I win or lose or draw, my nerve ends are all raw,
For the Prat really thinks, 'What a bum'.

So now, I will play, in an unsporting way
Using tricks you will not find in a book.
And all players will say 'The stupid sod still can't play,
And more than that, he's now a cheating rotten crook.'
And everyone will know my name, as I strive to seek acclaim
Using tactics in a most unsporting way.
And with a skin that's not so thin, I'll ignore the boos and
  raucous din,
That will echo round the 'Greens' whereon I play.

And in the seasons yet to come, no one will say that I'm a bum
For I'll be playing like a nutter gone astray,
And when the bowling seasons done, I will be 'The Number One',
But all my friends will have quietly walked away.
Now you all know, it's just a joke, for I'm a really friendly bloke
And the words you've read were written just for fun,
There is no way I could play, in such a fearful craven way
And so it's back to being known as 'Last but One'.

My Prayer

Thank you dear God for another day,
Thank you for my work and play.
Please grant to me a peaceful night,
That I may wake at morning light
Refreshed in mind and spirit too,
Ready to do my best for you.